THE STORY OF ME AND MY

First published by Parragon Books Ltd in 2013
LIFE CANVAS is an imprint of Parragon Books Ltd

Parragon
Chartist House
15-17 Trim Street
Bath BA1 1HA, UK
www.parragon.com

Produced by Tall Tree Ltd
Illustrations by Apple Agency

ISBN 978-1-4723-0742-2
GTIN 5060292801025

Printed in China

A LETTER TO DAD ABOUT THIS BOOK

Date ....

Dear Dad,

love from...

where ....

when ....

JUST THE
TWO OF US

OUR JOURNEY TOGETHER

IF YOU FOLLOW THIS THREAD
THROUGH THE BOOK, YOU'LL SEE
PHOTOS, SOME OLD AND SOME
NEW, SOME OF YOU, SOME OF ME,
AND SOME OF US TOGETHER.

stick your photo here

ALL ABOUT MY DAD

Dad's favorite color ....

Dad's dream car ....

Dad's favorite song ....

Dad's best friend ....

Dad's favorite TV show ....

Dad's dream vacation ....

Dad likes to eat ....

Dad likes to play ....

LOVE THE SONG OR HATE IT?

song

Dad does this
when it's playing

1. .... a b c

2. .... a b c

3. .... a b c

4. .... a b c

5. .... a b c

a. Dances like a crazy person b. Won't move from his chair c. Turns it off

DAD AND I LAUGHED
SO MUCH WHEN...

Dad likes to do these things...*

	really likes	likes	pretends to like	dislikes
Watching TV	☐	☐	☐	☐
Going to work	☐	☐	☐	☐
Lying around	☐	☐	☐	☐
Cooking	☐	☐	☐	☐
Shopping online	☐	☐	☐	☐
Fixing things	☐	☐	☐	☐
Working out	☐	☐	☐	☐
Playing on a games console	☐	☐	☐	☐
Shopping with Mom	☐	☐	☐	☐
Cutting the grass	☐	☐	☐	☐
Meeting friends	☐	☐	☐	☐
Watching sports	☐	☐	☐	☐
Playing games with me	☐	☐	☐	☐
Cooking on the grill	☐	☐	☐	☐
....	☐	☐	☐	☐
....	☐	☐	☐	☐
....	☐	☐	☐	☐
....	☐	☐	☐	☐

*Does he really?

stick your photo here

YOU ALWAYS SAY THIS

THINGS YOU'VE
TAUGHT ME

✓

How to throw a ball ☐
How to ride a bike ☐
How to start a barbecue ☐
How to cast a fishing rod ☐
How to tie my shoelaces ☐
How to fix breakfast ☐
How to make my bed ☐

.... ☐
.... ☐
.... ☐
.... ☐
.... ☐
.... ☐

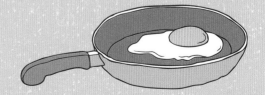

Remember when?

Use this space to write about something that happened to you and your Dad.

....

....

....

....

....

....

....

....

....

....

....

....

....

....

....

....

....

....

WHEN WE GO OUT TO EAT DAD ALWAYS ORDERS

Appetizer

Main course

Dessert

Delivery available • Service not included • Private parties catered for

stick your photo here

YOU EMBARRASSED ME WHEN...

WHEN I DO THESE THINGS
IT MAKES YOU
MAD

1. ....
2. ....
3. ....
4. ....
5. ....

IF NO ONE TOLD YOU WHAT TO WEAR...

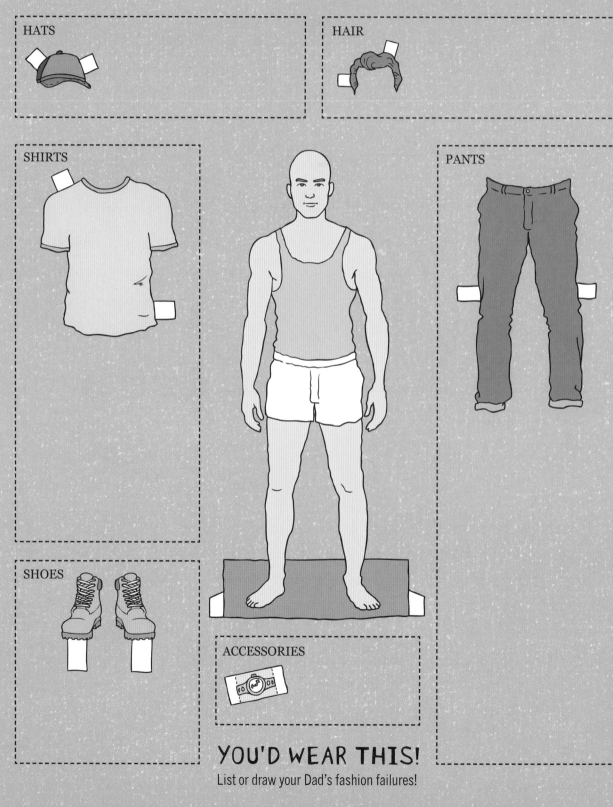

HATS

HAIR

SHIRTS

PANTS

SHOES

ACCESSORIES

YOU'D WEAR THIS!

List or draw your Dad's fashion failures!

MY FAVORITE THINGS
TO DO WITH YOU

DAD'S FAVORITE
GADGETS

Circle the smile rating that matches your Dad.

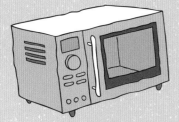

Dad's rating

Remote control	☺	☺	⊖	☹	☹
Cell phone	☺	☺	⊖	☹	☹
Microwave	☺	☺	⊖	☹	☹
Power drill	☺	☺	⊖	☹	☹
E-reader	☺	☺	⊖	☹	☹
TV	☺	☺	⊖	☹	☹
Computer	☺	☺	⊖	☹	☹
G.P.S.	☺	☺	⊖	☹	☹
MP3 player	☺	☺	⊖	☹	☹
Camera	☺	☺	⊖	☹	☹
Games console	☺	☺	⊖	☹	☹
....	☺	☺	⊖	☹	☹

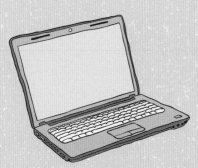

Stick in your favorite photo of you and your Dad doing one of your favorite things.

You like to watch these TV shows...

but do I?

	really likes	likes	pretends to like	dislikes
....	☐	☐	☐	☐
....	☐	☐	☐	☐
....	☐	☐	☐	☐
....	☐	☐	☐	☐

I like to watch these TV shows...

but do you?

	really likes	likes	pretends to like	dislikes
....	☐	☐	☐	☐
....	☐	☐	☐	☐
....	☐	☐	☐	☐
....	☐	☐	☐	☐

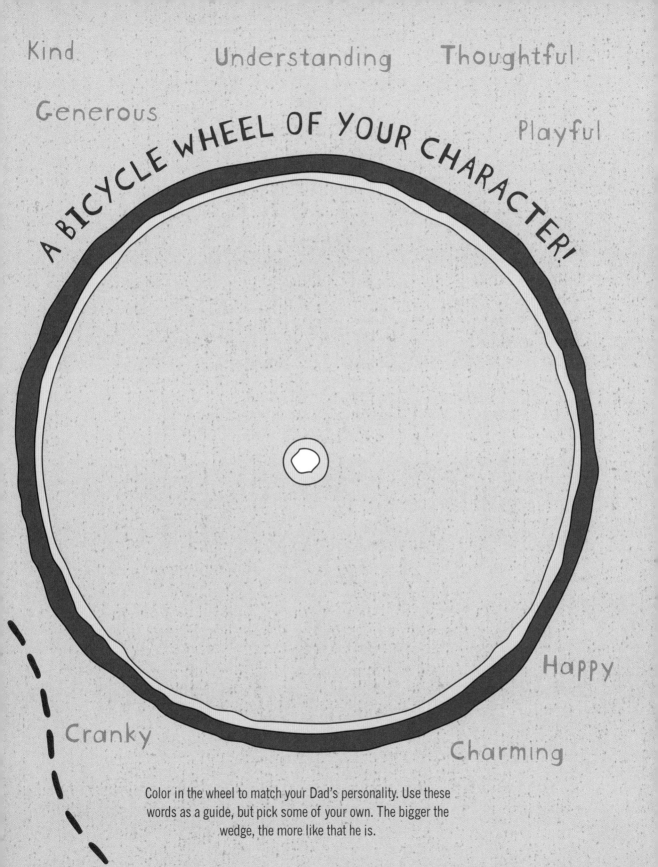

Kind Understanding Thoughtful

Generous Playful

A BICYCLE WHEEL OF YOUR CHARACTER!

Happy

Cranky Charming

Color in the wheel to match your Dad's personality. Use these words as a guide, but pick some of your own. The bigger the wedge, the more like that he is.

Dad's best jokes

....
....
....
....
....
....
....
....
....

Dad's worst jokes

....
....
....
....
....
....
....
....
....

stick your photo here

MY DAD'S THE BEST BECAUSE...

....
....
....
....
....
....
....
....
....

1st

SAY IT WITH PICTURES

Say it with pictures instead of words and see if Dad
knows what you're saying!

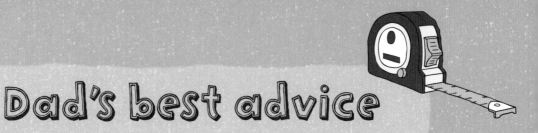

Dad's best advice

....
....
....
....
....
....
....
....

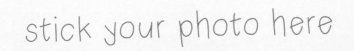

stick your photo here

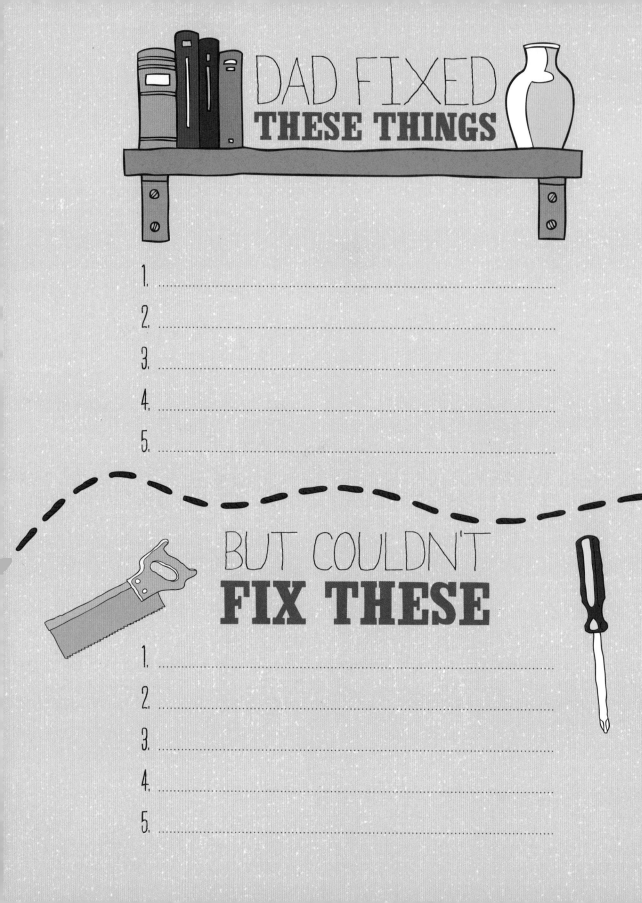

DAD FIXED THESE THINGS

1. ....
2. ....
3. ....
4. ....
5. ....

BUT COULDN'T FIX THESE

1. ....
2. ....
3. ....
4. ....
5. ....

Things Dad Dislikes

- [ ] Asking for directions
- [ ] Swimming
- [ ] Watching reality TV
- [ ] Doing the laundry
- [ ] Going shopping
- [ ] Playing board games
- [ ] Washing the dishes
- [ ] Driving me around

- [ ] ....
- [ ] ....
- [ ] ....

THE JUDGING PANEL
GAVE YOU THESE
SCORES OUT OF 10

Dress sense

Creativity

Craziness

Patience

Music you listen to

Cheerfulness

Thoughtfulness

Generosity

Score Dad from 0–10 on the judges' paddles.

IF EVERY DAY WAS
FATHER'S
DAY
WE WOULD

....
....
....
....
....
....
....
....

YOU MAKE ME
MAD WHEN...

....
....
....
....
....

where ....
when ....

I WISH I'D TAKEN A PICTURE WHEN

Draw a missed photo opportunity in the frame below.

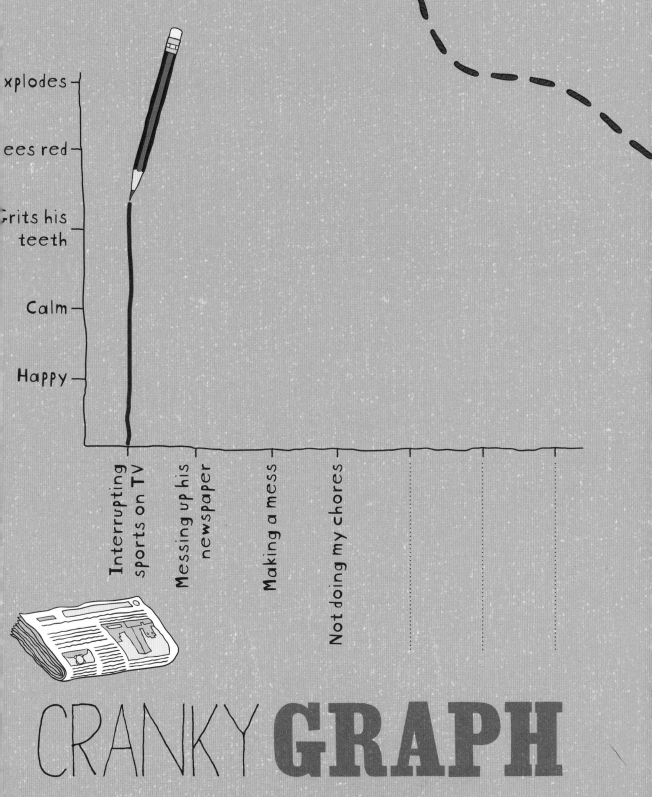

CRANKY GRAPH

Complete this line graph to see how cranky Dad is.

CAUGHT ON CAMERA
Dad not looking his best

where ....

when ....

PLEASE DON'T EVER DANCE TO
THESE SONGS IN PUBLIC...

1. ....
2. ....
3. ....
4. ....
5. ....

...AND DON'T SING THESE SONGS
OUT LOUD EITHER!

1. ....
2. ....
3. ....
4. ....
5. ....

Rating Dad's skills

Circle the face that best shows how good your Dad is at...

Fixing things ☹ 😐 ☺   Listening ☹ 😐 ☺

Singing ☹ 😐 ☺   Telling stories ☹ 😐 ☺

Dancing ☹ 😐 ☺   Playing sports ☹ 😐 ☺

Cleaning ☹ 😐 ☺   .... ☹ 😐 ☺

Telling jokes ☹ 😐 ☺   .... ☹ 😐 ☺

Driving ☹ 😐 ☺   .... ☹ 😐 ☺

Cooking ☹ 😐 ☺   .... ☹ 😐 ☺

Giving hugs ☹ 😐 ☺   .... ☹ 😐 ☺

- [ ] Play a board game
- [ ] Wash your car
- [ ] Go to the beach
- [ ] Watch a game on TV
- [ ] Go on an outdoor adventure
- [ ] Go to the movies
- [ ] Play baseball
- [ ] Ride our bikes
- [ ] ....
- [ ] ....
- [ ] ....
- [ ] ....

WHAT SHOULD WE DO TOGETHER?

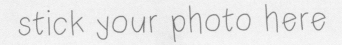

stick your photo here

....
....
....
....
....
....
....
....

our best
FAMILY VACATION

1. ....
2. ....
3. ....
4. ....
5. ....

DAD'S HEROES!

List the top five people your
Dad admires most.

What we have in common

Me

Dad

I'M JUST LIKE YOU!

WE NEARLY GOT INTO TROUBLE
WITH MOM WHEN WE...

stick your photo here

MY FAVORITE
ADVENTURE WITH YOU

things to do
ON A RAINY DAY

I promise to...

1. ....
   ....

2. ....
   ....

3. ....
   ....

4. ....
   ....

5. ....
   ....

LAUGH-O-METER

Complete this bar chart to see how funny Dad is at...

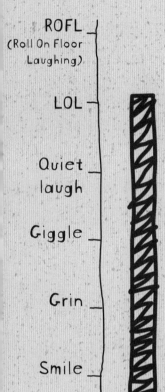

ROFL
(Roll On Floor
Laughing)

LOL

Quiet
laugh

Giggle

Grin

Smile

Funny dancing

Telling jokes

WE MUST DO
these things together

....
....
....
....
....
....
....
....
....
....
....
....
....
....
....

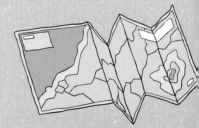

WHY YOU MEAN THE WORLD TO ME

THIS IS US NOW